Happy Birthday
Gerri

from

your friend Diane

D1113532

The Gardener's
Guide to Life

The Gardener's Guide to Life

Timeless Lessons Based on the Principles of Gardening

Compiled and Edited by Criswell Freeman

WALNUT GROVE PRESS
Nashville, TN 37205

ISBN 1-887655-40-9

The ideas expressed in this book are not, in all cases, exact quotations, as some have been edited for clarity and brevity. In all cases, the author has attempted to maintain the speaker's original intent. In some cases, material for this book was obtained from secondary sources, primarily print media. While every effort was made to ensure the accuracy of these sources, the accuracy cannot be guaranteed. For additions, deletions, corrections or clarifications in future editions of this text, please write WALNUT GROVE PRESS.

Printed in the United States of America
Cover Design by Mary Mazer
Typesetting & Page Layout by Sue Gerdes
Editor for Walnut Grove Press: Alan Ross
1 2 3 4 5 6 7 8 9 10 • 97 98 99 00 01

ACKNOWLEDGMENTS
The author gratefully acknowledges the helpful support of Angela Beasley, Dick and Mary Freeman, Mary Susan Freeman, Jim Gallery, and Sue Hunt.

For Harvey and Dick Freeman

A Fruitful Partnership

Table of Contents

Introduction

In 1959, when I was five years old, my father introduced me to the joys of gardening. Dad took me aside, put his hand on my shoulder, and gave me an important assignment: growing the family radishes. Then he marked off a few square feet of his garden, helped me with the planting, and answered my questions. The rest, he said, was up to me.

The responsibility of my duties seemed overwhelming at first, but I weeded, watered, and prayed. Thankfully, Mother Nature did her part; we enjoyed a bountiful crop, and I acquired a taste for homegrown vegetables. More importantly, I learned invaluable lessons about life. That garden was a wonderful learning laboratory. It still is.

This book celebrates the gentle wisdom of gardening through the words of philosophers, poets, naturalists and, above all, gardeners. The ideas herein, while not new, are profoundly important because success in the garden — or out — depends upon certain unchanging principles.

If you're ready to get your hands dirty and dig for insights about land and life, turn the page. But first, would anyone care for some good homegrown radishes?

1

Gratitude

Cicero observed, "A thankful heart is not only the greatest virtue, but the parent of all other virtues." Nowhere is a thankful heart more appropriate than in a garden.

Whether it's a two-acre behemoth or a midtown window box, a garden is a place where the majesty of creation is revealed each day. Mother Nature works her miracles as Father Time marks the cycle of life; meanwhile, the observant gardener witnesses a show like no other. And the price of admission is a bargain: a plot of ground, a ray of hope, and a handful of seeds.

Sometimes, a garden can be a frustrating place. Plants can be stubborn, pests can be persistent, and weather can be uncooperative. When things begin to grow wrong, so do emotions; but no one should work the soil in anger.

So the next time you find yourself muttering about weeds, weather or bugs, pause to give thanks for your garden; it's a gift from God that keeps on giving. As such, we gardeners are advised to keep on thanking.

No occupation is so delightful to me as the culture of the earth, and no culture comparable to that of the garden.

Thomas Jefferson

The gardening bug can bite at any moment.
Barbara Damrosch

Gardening is a kind of self-prescribed
preventative medicine, good for all ills.
Sheryl London

To own a bit of ground, to scratch it
with a hoe, to plant seeds, and watch their
renewal of life — this is the commonest
delight of the race, the most satisfactory
thing a man can do.
Charles Dudley Warner

The garden is a love song, a duet between
a human being and Mother Nature.
Jeff Cox

Gratitude

Love of gardening is a seed that once sown
never dies.

Gertrude Jekyll

Each day comes bearing its own gifts.
Untie the ribbons.

Ruth Ann Schabacker

Man is happy in a garden because God
has made him so and to live in a garden is the
nearest he can reach to paradise on earth.

Nan Fairbrother

In a thousand unseen ways we have drawn
shape and strength from the land.

Lyndon B. Johnson

Nobody can be in good health
if he does not have all the time, fresh air,
sunshine, and good water.

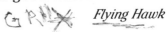 *Flying Hawk*

This used to be among my prayers —
a piece of land not so very large, which would
contain a garden, and near the house a spring
of everflowing water, and beyond these a bit
of wood.

Horace

I find the love of garden grows upon me
more and more as I grow older.

Maria Edgeworth

More and more I feel the need for a house
with a garden.

Marie Curie

I have often thought that if heaven had given
me choice of my position and calling, it
should have been on a rich spot of earth, well
watered, and near a good market for the
productions of the garden.

Thomas Jefferson

I look upon the pleasure which we take
in a garden as one of the most innocent
delights in human life.

Cicero

Gratitude

Who loves a garden still his Eden keeps,
Perennial pleasures plants and
wholesome harvest reaps.

Bronson Alcott

He who receives a benefit with gratitude
repays the first installment on his debt.

Marcus Annaeus Seneca

Thanksgiving was never meant to be shut up
in a single day.

Robert Caspar Lintner

In the beginning God created the heavens and
the earth ... God saw all that He had made,
and it was very good.

Genesis 1: 1, 31

God almighty first planted a garden. And,
indeed, it is the purest of human pleasures.

Francis Bacon

One is nearer God's heart in a garden than anywhere else on earth.

Dorothy Frances Gurney

Gratitude

One should learn also to enjoy
the neighbor's garden, however small;
the roses straggling over the fence, the scent
of lilacs drifting across the road.

Henry Van Dyke

If you have never had a garden, you cannot
understand, and if you have had a garden,
you will know that it would take a whole book
to describe all that came to pass there.

Frances Hodgson Burnett

Gardening has compensations out of all
proportion to its goals. It is creation
in the pure sense.

Phyllis McGinley

The unthankful heart discovers no mercies;
but the thankful heart will find, in every hour,
some heavenly blessings!

Henry Ward Beecher

There is nothing pleasanter than spading
when the ground is soft and damp.

John Steinbeck

What I enjoy is not the fruits alone,
but I also enjoy the soil itself.

Cicero

Cultivate a thankful spirit! It will be to you
a perpetual feast.

John R. MacDuff

We are thankful to Thee for sunshine
and rain and also for health and strength
to enable us to work with Nature
"from dawn to the setting sun."

Jim G. Brown's Garden Prayer for 1945

Thanksgiving invites God to bestow
a second benefit.

Robert Herrick

To live happily is an inward power of the soul.
Marcus Aurelius

Happiness and misery depend as much
on temperament as on fortune.
La Rochefoucauld

He who plants a garden plants happiness.
Chinese Proverb

Live now, believe me, wait not till tomorrow;
gather the roses of life today.
Pierre de Ronsard

Happiness is a habit. Cultivate it.
Elbert Hubbard

If you want to be happy for an hour, have a party. If you want to be happy for a week, kill your pig and eat it. But if you want to be happy all your life, become a gardener.

Chinese Saying

You're only here for a short visit. Don't hurry, don't worry, and stop to smell the flowers along the way.

Walter Hagen

2

Planning

"Plan your work, then work your plan" is a bit of advice we have all heard over and over. But reminders about the importance of planning are always worth repeating, especially to gardeners.

Alexander Pope wrote, "All gardening is landscape painting." Before you begin *your* masterpiece, reduce it to paper. Consider such matters as design, climate, sunlight, and, above all, your own tastes. Thoughtful preparation will pay more dividends than a wheelbarrow full of fertilizer, so remember: Plan your work, *then* work your plants.

Order is heaven's first law.

Alexander Pope

Too often gardeners start with seed
instead of graph paper.

Helen Van Pelt Wilson

Planning a garden on paper is simple —
but important.

Jamie Jobb

Plan your garden on paper.
Mistakes made on paper won't cost
you much in either time or money.

Elsa Bakalar

Mishaps can be avoided by advance
planning, without taking any of the fun out
of gardening.

Barbara Damrosch

The noble man makes noble plans,
and by noble deeds he stands.

Isaiah 32: 8

Planning

Although much of the pleasure in gardening
derives from serendipitous effects,
thorough planning is essential.

Tom Wright

The plans of the diligent lead to profit.

Proverbs 21: 5

Think about the garden as a small community
of plants and animals coexisting with
one another and with human beings.

Ruth Shaw Ernst

Well-balanced gardens have a quality
of restfulness and exquisite perfection,
with plants chosen and placed like words
in a perfect poem.

Jeff Cox

The essence of the enjoyment of a garden
is that things should look as though they like
to grow in it.

Beatrix Farrand

Finding a place for a garden can be just like
a treasure hunt.

Sheryl London

Anywhere you live you can find room
for a garden somewhere.

 Jamie Jobb

As you plan your garden, consider the
element of time. The flowers that bloom in
May will not be blooming in August.

Barbara Damrosch

No two gardens are exactly alike.

Felicity Bryan

There is a style of garden to suit
every personality.

Tom Wright

Nature does not complete things.
She is chaotic. Man must finish, and he does
so by making a garden and building a wall.

Robert Frost

Nature goes her own way, and all that
to us seems an exception is really according
to order.

Goethe

Nature, to be commanded, must be obeyed.

Francis Bacon

 ${A}$ plant is like a self-willed man,
 out of whom we can obtain all which we
desire, if we will only treat him his own way.

Goethe

 ${M}$ an masters nature not by force
 but by understanding.

Dad · Mitchell

Jacob Bronowski

 ${T}$ he first rule of successful gardening is
to work with, not against, the natural setting.

Burpee Complete Gardener

Gardening is a form of art which everyone,
rightly or wrongly, considers to be
within his talents.

Anonymous

If you garden you think about gardens.
Ideas keep manifesting themselves, they seep
into your mind often when you are
nowhere near a garden.

Mirabel Osler

To make a great garden, one must have
a great idea or a great opportunity.

Sir George Sitwell

All gardens are a form of autobiography.

Robert Dash

As is the gardener, so is the garden.

Old Saying

Good planning takes many other factors
into account besides plant choices, including
soil building, sun, shade, and plant placement.

Ruth Shaw Ernst

It is not possible to use to any good effect
all the plants there are to be had.

Gertrude Jekyll

A place for everything,
everything in its place.

Ben Franklin

Your garden plan should leave room
for expansion.

Mary Deputy Cassell

Nothing is more completely the child of art
than a garden.

Sir Walter Scott

A gardener is the spirit of the garden, the organizing force, the heart and soul of it all.

Jeff Cox

Deciding what to grow is one of the most enjoyable aspects of gardening.

Burpee Complete Gardener

Climate is the single-most important factor in how plants grow — indeed in what we select to plant in the first place.

Jack Kramer

Remember the end, and thou shalt never do amiss.

Ecclesiasticus

The wise gardener
anticipates June
in January.

House and Garden

Beware of starting what you may later regret.
Publilius Syrus

Even the best plan degenerates into work.
Anonymous

Begin. To begin is half the work.
Ausonius

Once you've finalized your plan,
it's time to get your hands dirty.
Burpee Complete Gardener

3

Diligence

Gardening, like life, rewards diligence. More often than not, the soil is fair: the size of one's harvest tends to be proportional to the size of one's efforts.

Thankfully, the work of gardening isn't really work in the strictest sense. The experience of digging in the moist earth is sublime pleasure. Still, this pleasure is not optional for the man or woman who expects a bumper crop.

Gardening may be a labor of love, but it is still labor. The self-tending garden has yet to be invented. Hopefully, it never will be. After all, what would a garden be without the work of gardening? A grocery store.

True!

Geraldine Ruby Mitchell -
Palajac - Hamilton.
Nov. 30 . 2015
X O

The spontaneous
energies of the earth
are a gift of nature,
but they require the
labors of man to direct
their operation.

Thomas Jefferson

We are here to cultivate the garden
and take care of it.

Genesis 2: 15

He who would eat the fruit
must climb the tree.

Scottish Proverb

To have the harvest we must sow the seed.

Liberty Hyde Bailey

Never is work without reward
or reward without work.

Livy

Gardens are not made by singing,
"Oh, how beautiful," and sitting in the shade.

Rudyard Kipling

Diligence

Show me your garden and I shall tell you
what you are.

Alfred Austin

Did you ever think how a bit of land
displays the character of the owner?

Laura Ingalls Wilder

Die when I may, I want it said by those
who knew me best, that I always plucked
a thistle and planted a flower where I thought
a flower would grow.

Abraham Lincoln

What this country needs is dirtier fingernails
and cleaner minds.

Will Rogers

Whatsoever a man soweth, that shall he also reap.

Galatians 6: 7

There is a common error of thought that all virgin soils are necessarily good. Nature laid down her soil in a haphazard way.

Louis Bromfield

The farmer who takes everything
from the land without restitution
will become the servant of wiser men,
either on the farm or elsewhere.

C. E. Thorne

Babylon died because its soil died.

The Nashville Tennessean

Put in the plow and plant the great hereafter
in the now.

Robert Browning

Every gardener knows that one of the
chief joys of his activity is working deeply
with the soil, pushing one's hands deep
into its moist, life-giving crumbliness.

Jeff Cox

First prepare a deep, loose seedbed,
and then don't walk on it.

Dick Raymond

Working in the garden gives me something
beyond the enjoyment of the senses. It gives
me a profound feeling of inner peace.

Ruth Stout

The highest reward for man's toil is not what
he gets for it but what he becomes by it.

John Ruskin

My good hoe as it bites the ground
revenges my wrongs, and I have less lust
to bite my enemies. In smoothing
the rough hillocks, I smooth my temper.

Ralph Waldo Emerson

What is it about gardening that works out
something bad?

Anne Chotzinoff Grossman

We have no time to sin when we devote
our time to working in the garden with God.

Jim G. Brown

From labor comes health; from health,
contentment springs.

James Beattie

Happiness is activity.

Aristotle

After the fine exercise in the garden,
I have an appetite like a 12-year-old
and have no sleepless nights.

Jim G. Brown

Sloth makes all things difficult
but industry all things easy.

Ben Franklin

Choose a job you love, and you will never
work a day in your life.

Confucius

No garden is without weeds.

Thomas Fuller

What is a weed? For me, a weed is a plant
out of place.

Donald Culross Peattie

What is a weed? A plant whose virtues
have not yet been discovered.

Ralph Waldo Emerson

A weed is no more than a flower in disguise.

James Russell Lowell

I guess a good gardener starts
as a good weeder.

Amos Pettingill

Weed your own garden first.

Old Saying

Thank God every morning when you get up
that you have something to do that day which
must be done, whether you like it or not.

Charles Kingsley

Where our work is, there let our joy be.

Tertullian

A man's best friends are his ten fingers.

Robert Collyear

In order to live off the garden,
you practically have to live in it.

Kin Hubbard

Diligence

Though the wide universe is full of good,
no kernel of nourishing corn can come to him
but through his toil bestowed on that plot of
ground which is given to him to till.

Ralph Waldo Emerson

Plough deep while sluggards sleep; and you
shall have corn to sell and to keep.

Ben Franklin

He who tills his land will have plenty of food.

Proverbs 28: 19

Those who labor in the earth
are the chosen people of God.

Thomas Jefferson

4

Attention

Attention is as critical to good gardening as water or fertilizer. All plants exist in a state of constant change, so wise gardeners work with their eyes as well as their hands.

As we attend to our gardens, we notice small problems before they grow into big ones. But more importantly, we witness a timeless drama that is played out between plant, animal, earth and man.

Ralph Waldo Emerson wrote, "The landscape belongs to the person who looks at it." Emerson understood that the beauty of nature should never be taken for granted.

Every garden presents an amazing visual show. The more closely we observe, the more bountiful our rewards. No wonder the best gardens are carefully watched.

One of the most important things a gardener does is *look*. The rewards are immeasurable.

Elsa Bakalar

See Nature, and through her, God.

Henry David Thoreau

Never lose an opportunity of seeing anything that is beautiful, for beauty is God's handwriting — a wayside sacrament.

Ralph Waldo Emerson

Nature will bear the closest inspection. She invites us to lay our eye level with her smallest leaf, and take an insect's view of its plain.

Henry David Thoreau

Nobody sees a flower — really — it's so small. It takes time — we haven't time — and to see takes time, like to have a friend takes time.

Georgia O'Keeffe

Awareness of the continuous process
of birth, growth, bloom, death, decay, and
renewal gives rise to a feeling of kinship
with all living things.

Ruth Shaw Ernst

To my mind, there is nothing to beat
personal observations and visits to gardens.

Rosemary Verey

Tranquil, harmonious observations nourish
and refresh the mind. This, too, is part of the
naturalist's garden.

Ruth Shaw Ernst

Flowers are like human beings.
They thrive on a little kindness.

Fred Streeter

To get the best results, you must talk
to your vegetables.

Prince Charles

To him who in the love of nature holds
communion with her visible forms,
she speaks a various language.

William Cullen Bryant

Beauty is God's handwriting.
Welcome it in every fair face, every fair sky,
every fair flower.

Charles Kingsley

Nature is painting for us, day after day,
pictures of infinite beauty if only we have
the eyes to see them.

John Ruskin

Beauty can inspire miracles.

Benjamin Disraeli

A thing of beauty is a joy forever.

John Keats

No place on earth is more sensuous
than a garden.

Jeff Cox

There is something about sun and soil that
heals broken bodies and jangled nerves
Nature Magazine

Most people don't see the sun, soil, bugs,
seeds, plants, moon, water, clouds, and wind
the way gardeners do.

Jamie Jobb

We do not see nature with our eyes,
but with our understanding and our hearts.

William Hazlitt

When I first open my eyes upon
the morning meadows and look out upon the
beautiful world, I thank God I am alive.

Ralph Waldo Emerson

Attention

How cunningly nature hides every wrinkle
of her inconceivable antiquity under roses and
violets and morning dew!

Ralph Waldo Emerson

Most human beings have an almost infinite
capacity for taking things for granted.

Aldous Huxley

A man who never sees a bluebird
only half lives.

Lewis Gannett

He who has been instructed in the things of
love, and who has learned to see the beautiful
in due order and succession, when he comes
toward the end will suddenly perceive
a nature of wondrous beauty.

Plato

The breath of flowers is far sweeter in the air
than in the hand.

Francis Bacon

Nothing awakens
a reminiscence
like an odor.

Victor Hugo

Our notion of what makes a paradise
always returns to the image of a beautiful and
fruitful garden.

Jeff Cox

To see a world in a grain of sand and heaven
in a wild flower; hold infinity in the palm
of your hand and eternity in an hour.

William Blake

One by one our senses are captivated and
charmed by the garden and then all together:
We are swimming in birdsong and perfume,
fresh flavor and cool touches, all decorated
with gorgeous colors.

Jeff Cox

Almost any garden, if you see it at just the
right moment, can be confused with paradise.

Henry Mitchell

5

Silence

Silence is one of the most endearing qualities of a garden. As Oliver Wendell Holmes observed, "Silence, like a poultice, comes to heal the blows of sound."

The next time you visit your chosen patch of soil, listen to the gentle sounds of nature. A quiet garden is guaranteed to restore perspective and nourish the soul.

Silence

Silence is deep as eternity.
Speech is shallow as time.

Thomas Carlyle

God is the friend of silence. Trees, flowers,
grass grow in silence. See the stars, moon,
and sun, how they move in silence.

Mother Teresa

The silence of nature is very real.
It surrounds you. You can feel it.

Ted Trueblood

Silence is a great peacemaker.

Henry Wadsworth Longfellow

Silence is a friend who will never betray.

Confucius

Nothing in all creation is so like God as stillness.

Meister Eckhart

Silence

Silence is full of potential wisdom.

Aldous Huxley

In quietness and in confidence shall be
your strength.

Ralph Waldo Emerson

A happy life must be to a great extent
a quiet life, for it is in an atmosphere
of quiet that true joy can live.

Bertrand Russell

Quiet places should be enjoyed.
Save the quiet places first.

Ernest Lyons

Flowers and plants are silent presences;
   they nourish every sense but the ear.

Mary Sarton

Flowers are our greatest silent friends.

Jim G. Brown

Silence is but a rich pause in the music
   of life.

Sarojini Naidu

True joy is serene.

Marcus Annaeus Seneca

One of the most soothing sounds of nature
is the laughter of falling water.

Jeff Cox

The most sublime state a human being
can aspire to is being in the wilderness alone
with God.

Malcolm Muggeridge

I love to be alone. I never found
the companion that was so companionable
as solitude.

Henry David Thoreau

Creating a garden is like making music:
The least distraction is apt to destroy
the melodic line.

Beverly Nichols

The early morning has gold in its mouth.

Ben Franklin

Never give up listening to the sounds
of birds.

John James Audubon

We need the tonic of the wilderness.

Henry David Thoreau

Everything true and great grows in silence.
Without silence we fall short of reality and
cannot plumb the depths of being.

Ladislaus Boros

The hills are mute, but how they speak of God!

Charles Hansom Towne

The present state of the world and the whole
of life is diseased. If I were a doctor and
were asked for my advice, I should reply:
Create silence.

Søren Kierkegaard

Discover
creative solitude.

Carl Sandburg

Silence is the element
in which great things
fashion themselves.

Thomas Carlyle

6

Optimism

Gardeners are, by nature, an optimistic lot. They gladly sink money, effort and time into a plot of ground with no guarantee of return. Planting a garden is truly faith in action.

In this chapter, we consider one of the gardener's most useful tools: a highly cultivated sense of optimism. Why is an upbeat attitude so essential? Because in the garden, there are too many other things to worry about without adding the self-fulfilling prophecy to the list.

If you're a gardener — or if you're not — sow seeds of optimism. They're guaranteed to sprout.

Optimism is the faith that leads
to achievement. Nothing can be done
without hope and confidence.

Helen Keller

Great hopes make great men.

Thomas Fuller

In the long run, the pessimist may be proved
to be right, but the optimist has a better time
on the trip.

Daniel L. Reardon

It doesn't hurt to be optimistic.
You can always cry later.

Lucimar Santos de Lima

Gardeners, I think, dream bigger dreams than emperors.

Mary Cantwell

Optimism

A good disposition is a virtue in itself,
and it is lasting.

Ovid

Hope of gain lessens pain.

Ben Franklin

He who seeks trouble always finds it.

English Proverb

By trusting in Thee, we know our labors
are not in vain and that our harvest is great.

Jim G. Brown's Garden Prayer for 1945

At the heart of gardening
there is a belief
in the miraculous.

Mirabel Osler

One of the most delightful things about a garden is the anticipation it provides.

W. E. Johns

Hope is a much greater stimulant
than any happiness.

Nietzsche

The pessimist sees the difficulty in every
opportunity; the optimist sees the
opportunity in every difficulty.

Lawrence Pearsall Jacks

Each of us makes his own weather and
determines the color of the skies in the
emotional universe which he inhabits.

Bishop Fulton J. Sheen

He who fears he shall suffer
already suffers what he fears.

Michel de Montaigne

Man is what he believes.

Anton Chekhov

Growing a garden and staying out in the
fresh air after office hours seemed to give me
the strength to meet all problems
with greater courage.

Jim G. Brown

In my garden, care stops at the gate
and gazes at me wistfully through the bars.

Alexander Smith

All my hurts my garden spade can heal.

Ralph Waldo Emerson

Dig for victory.

Jim G. Brown

The man who has planted
a garden feels that he has
done something for the
good of the whole world.

Charles Dudley Warner

This is the day which
the Lord hath made,
we will rejoice and
be glad in it.

Psalms 118: 24

7

Patience

In *The Count of Monte Cristo*, Alexandre Dumas wrote, "All human wisdom is summed up in two words: 'wait' and 'hope.'" Spoken like a true gardener. Mother Nature moves at her own pace and will not be hurried by fretful humans.

If you're anxious for a flower to bloom or a seedling to sprout, wait and hope. And while you're waiting, consider the following quotations.

Sweet flowers are slow and weeds make haste.

William Shakespeare

Adapt the pace of nature; her secret is patience.

Ralph Waldo Emerson

No great thing is created suddenly.

Epictetus

Genius is nothing but a great aptitude
for patience.

Ben Franklin

The greatest prayer is patience.

Buddha

There is more to life than increasing its speed.

Gandhi

There is nothing so bitter that a patient mind
cannot find some solace in it.

Marcus Annaeus Seneca

Patience is the companion of wisdom.

St. Augustine

Endurance is nobler than strength
and patience nobler than beauty.

John Ruskin

Patience and time do more
than strength or passion.

La Fontaine

Patience

Teach us, O Lord, the disciplines of patience,
for we find that to wait is often harder
than to work.

Peter Marshall

There is as much difference between genuine
patience and sullen endurance, as between
the smile of love and the malicious gnashing
of teeth.

W. S. Plummer

Patience is a bitter plant but it has sweet fruit.

German Proverb

If you enjoy fruit, pluck not the flower.

Old Saying

Bring forth fruit
with patience.

Luke 8: 15

Our real blessings often appear to us in the
shape of pains, losses, and disappointments;
but let us have patience, and we shall soon
see them in the proper figures.

Joseph Addison

There is no great achievement that is not
the result of patient working and waiting.

J. G. Holland

A good gardener does not expect miracles.

Jules Oravetz, Sr.

With plants, persuasion is better
than force.

Elsa Bakalar

Genius may conceive but patient labor
must consummate.

Horace Mann

An hour's hard digging is a good way
of getting one's mind back
in the right perspective.

Richard Briers

Gardening is the best therapy in the world.

C. Z. Guest

Patience is power; with time and patience the mulberry leaf becomes silk.

Chinese Proverb

8

Perseverance

American diplomat John Foster observed, "Perhaps perseverance has been the radical principle of every great character." And perhaps perseverance has been the radical principle of every great gardener.

Plants, weather, soil and bugs sometimes conspire to destroy the harvest. For those who work in the soil, adversity is unfortunate but inevitable. Experienced gardeners are not discouraged; they simply keep gardening.

If your quest for fertility has become an exercise in futility, don't give up. Keep your sense of humor. And plant persistently. Eventually, something good is bound to turn up.

Whatever you do, do it with purpose;
do it thoroughly, not superficially.

Lord Chesterfield

Patience and diligence, like faith,
move mountains.

William Penn

The block of granite which is an obstacle
in the pathway of the weak, becomes a
stepping-stone in the pathway of the strong.

Thomas Carlyle

Let us not be weary in well doing; for in
due season we shall reap, if we faint not.

Galatins 6: 9

If a tree dies, plant another in its place.

Linnaeus

Nature soon takes over if the gardener is absent.

Penelope Hobhouse

God helps those who persevere.

The Koran

I believe God intended for everybody to
have at least one acre. Of course, He expects
us to labor six days each week
if we are to prosper thereon.

Jim G. Brown

In everything worth having, even in pleasure,
there is a point of pain or tedium that must be
survived so that the pleasure may revive
and endure.

G. K. Chesterton

All that I have accomplished or expect
or hope to accomplish, has been and will be
by that plodding, patient, persevering
process of accretion which builds by
the ant-heap, particle by particle,
thought by thought, fact by fact.

Elihu Burritt

Perseverance

We think birds are valuable and keep
three birdbaths on our front and side lawns.
The birds no doubt destroy many
of the harmful insects.

Jim G. Brown

Fortunately for man, the insect world is
divided against itself. Far more than half
the insects prey upon other insects.

Edwin Way Teale

No matter how your garden grows,
you will need some tools to keep it going.

Jack Kramer

Man is a tool-using animal. Without tools
he is nothing. With tools he is all.

Thomas Carlyle

Basic to an integrated life is a dominant ideal. To plow a straight row one must keep his eye on the goal rather than the plow.

J. M. Price

Perseverance

Last night, there came a frost, which has
done great damage to my garden. It is sad
that Nature will play such tricks
with us poor mortals.

Nathaniel Hawthorne

Better the fruit lost than the tree.

Old Saying

The fair-weather gardener, who will do
nothing except when the wind and weather
and everything else are favorable, is never
a master of his craft.

Henry Ellacombe

Your job as gardener is to try to keep things
running smoothly for the plants and animals
that live in or visit your yard, whatever the
weather decides to do.

Ruth Shaw Ernst

The Gardener's Guide to Life

There is no spot of ground, however arid,
bare, or ugly, that cannot be tamed.

Gertrude Jekyll

The only thing different about having
a green thumb is that you don't get
discouraged by failure. When something
doesn't work, you try again.

Beth Weidner

The true gardener, like a true artist,
is never satisfied.

H. E. Bates

Failure is the path of least persistence.

Anonymous

Plodding wins the race.

Aesop

The garden that is finished is dead.

H. E. Bates

Be thou the rainbow to the storms of life!

Byron

Take nature's vagaries
and pranks in stride.

Ruth Shaw Ernst

A garden is a thing of
beauty and a job forever.

Richard Briers

9

Lifetime Learning

The Roman satirist Juvenal wrote, "Never does nature say one thing and wisdom another." He could have added that the more closely we examine the workings of nature, the more we learn. Thankfully, lessons are not restricted to horticulture.

Gardening is an educational process that lasts a lifetime. Its diploma consists of a green thumb, a happy heart and a permanently enlarged soul. If you're ready for an advanced degree, Mother Nature is anxious to teach. Her class is always in session.

Nature is always hinting at us.

Robert Frost

Listen to Nature's teachings.

William Cullen Bryant

Deviation from Nature is deviation
from happiness.

Samuel Johnson

Man is wise and constantly in quest
of more wisdom; but the ultimate wisdom,
which deals with beginnings, remains locked
in a seed.

Hal Borland

Nature's lessons will remain opaque as long
as we are full of our own ideas
and preconceptions.

Jeff Cox

True wisdom consists in not departing
from nature but in molding our conduct
according to her laws and model.
Marcus Annaeus Seneca

There is no other door to knowledge than
the door Nature opens.
Luther Burbank

Nature's instructions are always slow,
those of men are generally premature.
Rousseau

Study nature as the countenance of God.
Charles Kingsley

It is the marriage of the soul with Nature
that makes the intellect fruitful, and gives
birth to imagination.
Henry David Thoreau

To learn is a natural pleasure, not confined
to philosophers, but common to all men.

Aristotle

Wisdom is ofttimes nearer when we stoop
than when we soar.

William Wordsworth

A man's wisdom gives him patience.

Proverbs 19: 11

Man must go back to nature for information.

Thomas Paine

A modest garden
contains, for those who
know how to look and
to wait, more instruction
than a library.

Henri Frédéric Amiel

All gardeners know better
than other gardeners.

Chinese Proverb

The trouble with garden bugs is simple.
People don't know enough about them. Most
bugs in your garden are good for the garden.
Get to know them.

Jamie Jobb

As you learn more about gardening,
every new experience means more to you
and makes a long-lasting impression.

Rosemary Verey

Little flower — but if I could understand
what you are, root and all; then, all in all,
I should know what God and man is.

Alfred, Lord Tennyson

Gardening is an art which is learned
by practice, experience and sensible advice.

Jules Oravetz, Sr.

The life so short, the craft so long to learn.
This was said about literature, but it really
fits gardening better.

Henry Mitchell

The more one gardens, the more one learns;
and the more one learns, the more one
realizes how little one knows. I suppose
the whole of life is like that.

V. Sackville-West

Though an old man,
I am but a young gardener.

Thomas Jefferson

When all is said and done, even after 10,000 years of husbandry, we still have much to learn about what makes our gardens flourish.

Shelley Goldbloom

A gardener learns more in the mistakes than in the successes.

Barbara Dodge Borland

Who bends a knee when violets grow, a hundred secret things shall know.

Rachel Field

Man masters nature not by force but by understanding.

Jacob Bronowski

The two keys to success in gardening are understanding how plants grow and understanding how to provide them with a better home.

Sheryl London

There are always newer, easier, and better ways to grow a good garden, and I've spent a lifetime trying to find them.

Dick Raymond

Once you understand what makes plants tick, you'll understand what you need to do to help them grow.

Barbara Damrosch

I think there are as many kinds of gardening as of poetry.

Joseph Addison

The greatest service anyone can render his
country is to add a new plant to its culture.

Thomas Jefferson

The lesson I have thoroughly learnt,
and wish to pass on to others, is to know
the enduring happiness that the love
of a garden gives.

Gertrude Jekyll

I perhaps owe having become a painter
to flowers.

Claude Monet

Nothing is a better lesson in the knowledge
of plants than to sit down in front of them
and handle them and look them over just
as carefully as possible.

Gertrude Jekyll

There is not a sprig of grass that shoots
uninteresting to me.

Thomas Jefferson

Give me a spark of
Nature's fire.
That's all the
learning I desire.

Robert Burns

A garden is moved by influences you
cannot see, fully comprehend or control. You
are only part of the whole blooming thing.

Jamie Jobb

The most instructive experiences
are those of everyday life.

Nietzsche

We would be happy if we studied nature more
in natural things and acted according
to nature, whose rules are few, plain,
and most reasonable.

William Penn

Eventually, a gardener
becomes a philosopher.

Barbara Dodge Borland

The love of flowers is really the best teacher of how to grow and understand them.

Max Schling

Good gardening is very simple, really. You just have to think like a plant.

Barbara Damrosch

<u>10</u>

Time

The third chapter of Ecclesiastes reminds us that, "To every thing there is a season, and a time to every purpose under heaven." In the garden, each passing season has its own special beauty and its own special purpose.

In this chapter we consider the inexorable march of Father Time. His travels take him through every garden, and his message is clear: Sow, reap, and share while there is still time.

A garden is a link to the passing seasons.

Sheryl London

I hate to be reminded of the passage of time, and in a garden of flowers one can never escape from it.

E. V. Lucas

Here is the great mystery of life and growth: Everything is changing, growing, aiming at something, but silently, unboastfully, taking its time.

Ruth Stout

Things seem to move very slowly in a garden. But nothing ever remains the same.

Jamie Jobb

The Gardener's Guide to Life

Nature gives to every time and season
some beauties of its own; and from morning
to night, as from the cradle to the grave, is but
a succession of changes so gentle and easy
that we can scarcely mark their progress.

Charles Dickens

Every gardener knows under the cloak
of winter lies a miracle — a seed waiting
to sprout, a bulb opening to light, a bud strain-
ing to unfurl. And the anticipation nurtures our
dream.

Barbara Winkler

Come to the garden,
The soul's sweet bouquet
The flowers of tomorrow
Are in the seeds of today.

JoAnna O'Keefe

There are two seasonal diversions that can
ease the bite of any winter. One is the January
thaw. The other is the seed catalogues.

Hal Borland

Time

Timeliness is best in all matters.

Hesiod

Day's sweetest moments are at dawn.

Ella Wheeler Wilcox

More than half a century has passed,
  and yet each spring, when I wander into the
primrose wood, I see the pale yellow blooms
    and smell their sweetest scent —
  for a moment I am seven years old again
    wandering in the fragrant wood.

Gertrude Jekyll

Though nothing can bring back the hour
Of splendor in the grass, of glory in the flower;
    We will grieve not, rather find
    Strength in what remains behind.

William Wordsworth

It may be true time began
in a garden. It's time
the way God created it:
as servant, not master.

Emilie Barnes

No winter lasts forever, no spring skips
its turn. April is a promise that May
is bound to keep, and we know it.

Hal Borland

Gardening really has no beginning
and no end. In particular, pleasures of the
sense of smell really know no seasons.

Tovah Martin

No matter what changes take place
in the world, or in me, nothing ever seems
to disturb the face of spring.

E. B. White

I should like to enjoy this summer flower by
flower, as if it were to be the last one for me.

André Gide

Each day is born anew
for him who takes
it rightly.

James Russell Lowell

Oh, this is the joy
of the rose — that it
blooms and goes.

Willa Cather

11

Reverence

During World War II, Americans were encouraged to grow their own food, thus freeing up badly needed rations for military consumption. Soon, twenty million citizens were growing "victory gardens." In 1945, after a lengthy competition, a champion gardener was named: Jim G. Brown. Brown not only grew the fruits and vegetables that filled his family's table; he also grew the flowers that adorned it.

Mr. Brown explained, "Flowers supply our souls with the beauty that is necessary to keep our thoughts in tune with nature."

Another naturalist, Henry David Thoreau wrote, "Heaven is under our feet as well as over our heads." Thoreau approached nature as if he were entering a house of worship. So did Mr. Brown. And so should we.

Nature is the living, visible garment of God.

Goethe

Adam was a gardener,
and God who made him sees
that half a proper gardener's work
is done upon his knees.

Rudyard Kipling

Look through nature up to nature's God.

Alexander Pope

He who plants a garden works
hand in hand with God.

Malloch

Gardening is an instrument of grace.

Mary Sarton

Reverence

A gardener's relationship with the soil
is little short of a religious experience.

Bernard Schofield

Reverence is one of the signs of strength;
irreverence is one of the surest indications
of weakness.

Anonymous

No man will rise high who jeers
at sacred things.

Anonymous

The word "miracle" aptly describes a seed.

Jack Kramer

All of God's earth is holy ground.

Joaquin Miller

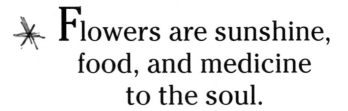 **F**lowers are sunshine,
food, and medicine
to the soul.

Luther Burbank

To create a little flower is the labour of ages.
William Blake

Flowers may beckon us, but they speak
toward heaven and God.
Henry Ward Beecher

Flowers are the sweetest things God ever
made and forgot to put a soul into.
Henry Ward Beecher

The amen of Nature is always a flower.
Oliver Wendell Holmes

Why are there trees I never walk under
but large and melodious thoughts
descend upon me?

Walt Whitman

Into every empty corner, into all forgotten
things and nooks, Nature struggles to pour life,
pouring life into the dead, life into life itself.

Henry Beston

Let all the earth fear the Lord; let all the
inhabitants of the world stand in awe of him.

Psalms 33: 8

The entire earth is a garden, a natural garden.

Jamie Jobb

One touch of nature
    makes the whole world kin.

William Shakespeare

Nature and the garden bring out the best
    in our characters.

Felicity Bryan

Happiness is a wayside flower growing
    upon the highways of usefulness.

Anonymous

Bloom where you're planted.

Mary Engelbreit

Reverence

What nature delivers to us is never stale,
because what nature creates has eternity in it.

Isaac Bashevis Singer

God, I can push the grass apart
And lay my finger on Thy heart!

Edna St. Vincent Millay

Bread feeds the body, but the flowers
feed the soul.

The Koran

The only words that ever satisfied me as
describing Nature are the terms used in fairy
books, "charm," "spell," "enchantment."

G. K. Chesterton

The soil is a wonderful thing.
Treat it like a good old friend.

Fred Streeter

Touch the earth, love the earth,
honour the earth.

Henry Beston

The tiny but significant part of the vast web
of life is the naturalist's garden.

Ruth Shaw Ernst

Confronted with the vision of a beautiful
garden, we see something beautiful about
ourselves, as a part of nature.

Jeff Cox

The Earth is our mother, She cares for us.
The Earth is our mother, we care for Her.

Native American Saying

Reverence

It is good to be alone in a garden at dawn
or dark so that all its shy presences may
haunt you and possess you in a reverie
of suspended thought.

James Douglas

Weather means more when you have
a garden. There's nothing like listening to a
shower and thinking how it is soaking in and
around your lettuce and green beans.

Marcelene Cox

Health, wealth and happiness will come
forth from Mother Earth if we diligently work
for the harvest.

Jim G. Brown

The best place to seek God is in a garden.
You can dig for him there.

George Bernard Shaw

Flowers are heaven's masterpieces.

Dorothy Parker

Consider the lilies of the field, how they grow; they toil not, neither do they spin. And yet I say unto you, that even Solomon in all his glory was not arrayed like one of these.

Matthew 6: 28-29

Behold! the Holy Grail is found,
Found in each poppy's cup of gold;
And God walks with us as of old.

Joaquin Miller

More than anything, I must have flowers, always, always.

Claude Monet

The best things that can come out
of any garden are gifts for other people.

Jamie Jobb

The best way to be thankful is to use
the goods the gods provide you.

Anthony Trollope

Flowers and fruits are always fit presents.

Ralph Waldo Emerson

Flowers leave some of their fragrance
in the hand that bestowed them.

Chinese Proverb

By their fruits ye shall know them.

Matthew 7: 20

Joy is the simplest form
of gratitude.

Karl Barth

Seeds of discouragement
will not grow in
a thankful heart.

Anonymous

The day, water, sun, moon, night — I do not have to purchase these things with money.

Plautus

I am in love with the green earth.

Charles Lamb

Whoever understands and loves a garden may have contentment if he will.

Chinese Proverb

Herbs are the friend of the physician
and the pride of cooks.

Charlemagne

The first gathering of salads, radishes and
herbs made me feel like a mother
about her baby — how could
anything so beautiful be mine?

Alice B. Toklas

At harvest time, the vegetable garden
comes into the kitchen. Not all at once,
unfortunately.

Barbara Dodge Borland

I grow my own vegetables for two reasons:
the quality of the crops I can produce myself,
and the quality of the time I spend doing it.

Barbara Damrosch

There is nothing that is comparable to it,
as satisfactory or as thrilling, as gathering
vegetables one has grown.

Alice B. Toklas

On Saturday evening, when we listen to the
radio and often shell dried beans, we are able
to relax after our week's work and realize
that there is more happiness in simple living
than in glamour.

Jim G. Brown

Amen! GRH

It's difficult to think anything but pleasant
thoughts while eating a homegrown tomato.

Lewis Grizzard

The greatest gift of a garden is the restoration
of the five senses.

Hanna Rion

It is a golden maxim to cultivate the garden
for the nose, and the eyes will take care
of themselves.

Robert Louis Stevenson

Flowers are the beautiful hieroglyphics
of nature with which she indicates how much
she loves us.

Goethe

A thing of beauty is a joy forever:
Its loveliness increases ...

John Keats

How fair is a garden amid the toils
and passions of existence.

Benjamin Disraeli

There was never a person who did anything
worth doing that did not receive more
than he gave.

Henry Ward Beecher

I want death to find me planting my cabbages.

Michel de Montaigne

A morning-glory at my window satisfies me
more than the metaphysics of books.

Walt Whitman

Arranging a bowl of flowers in the morning
can give a sense of quiet in a crowded day —
like writing a poem or saying a prayer.

Anne Morrow Lindbergh

"Just living is not enough," said the butterfly.
"One must have freedom, sunshine
and a little flower."

Hans Christian Anderson

The year's at the spring and day's at the morn;
Morning's at seven; The hillside's dew-pearled;
The lark's on the wing; The snail's on the thorn;
God's in His heaven — All's right with the world.

Robert Browning

Sources

Sources

Sources

About Wisdom Books

Wisdom Books chronicle memorable quotations in an easy-to-read style. Written by Criswell Freeman, this series provides inspiring, thoughtful and humorous messages from entertainers, athletes, scientists, politicians, clerics, writers and renegades. Each title focuses on a particular region or area of special interest.

Combining his passion for quotations with extensive training in psychology, Dr. Freeman revisits timeless themes such as perseverance, courage, love, forgiveness and faith.

"Quotations help us remember the simple yet profound truths that give life perspective and meaning," notes Freeman. "When it comes to life's most important lessons, we can all use gentle reminders."

About the Author

Criswell Freeman is a Doctor of Clinical Psychology living in Nashville, Tennessee. He is the author of *When Life Throws You a Curveball, Hit It* and *The Wisdom Series* from WALNUT GROVE PRESS.

The Wisdom Series

by Dr. Criswell Freeman

Regional Titles

Wisdom Made in America	ISBN 1-887655-07-7
The Book of Southern Wisdom	ISBN 0-9640955-3-X
The Wisdom of the Midwest	ISBN 1-887655-17-4
The Wisdom of the West	ISBN 1-887655-31-X
The Book of Texas Wisdom	ISBN 0-9640955-8-0
The Book of Florida Wisdom	ISBN 0-9640955-9-9
The Book of California Wisdom	ISBN 1-887655-14-X
The Book of New York Wisdom	ISBN 1-887655-16-6
The Book of New England Wisdom	ISBN 1-887655-15-8

Sports Titles

The Golfer's Book of Wisdom	ISBN 0-9640955-6-4
The Putter Principle	ISBN 1-887655-39-5
The Golfer's Guide to Life	ISBN 1-887655-38-7
The Wisdom of Southern Football	ISBN 0-9640955-7-2
The Book of Stock Car Wisdom	ISBN 1-887655-12-3
The Wisdom of Old-Time Baseball	ISBN 1-887655-08-5
The Book of Football Wisdom	ISBN 1-887655-18-2
The Book of Basketball Wisdom	ISBN 1-887655-32-8
The Fisherman's Guide to Life	ISBN 1-887655-30-1

Special Interest Titles

The Book of Country Music Wisdom	ISBN 0-9640955-1-3
The Wisdom of Old-Time Television	ISBN 1-887655-64-6
The Wisdom of the Heart	ISBN 1-887655-34-4
The Guide to Better Birthdays	ISBN 1-887655-35-2
The Gardener's Guide to Life	ISBN 1-887655-40-9
Minutes from the Great Women's Coffee Club (by Angela Beasley)	ISBN 1-887655-33-6

Wisdom Books are available through booksellers everywhere.
For information about a retailer near you, call 1-800-256-8584.